What's in my Powerpack?

Colour in or draw wherever you see this splat!

Your Powerpack has links to the web – look for the mouse.

Contents

About this...

Learn about the badges and awards you can get.

Make notes wherever you see the pencil.

Powerpack facts

Find out more about Cub Scouts with your Powerpack facts.

D0184018

All you need to know about Cub Scouts

Who are Cub Scouts?

Cub Scouts are people like you, usually aged between 8 – 10½. They meet together in Packs and take part in all sorts of activities.

As a Cub Scout you will:

→ have a lot of fun
→ try lots of new things
→ play games
→ make friends
→ explore your local area.

You may have swum up from Beaver Scouts and know a bit about Scouting already.

Or you may be new to Scouting. If you are, don't worry! You'll soon be having fun.

Where do I fit into the family of Scouting?

Cub Scouts are the second of five age groups. These age groups are called Sections. Can you see where you come in?

the Scout Network
age 18 – 25

Explorer Scouts
age 14 – 18

Scouts
age 10½ – 14

Cub Scouts
age 8 – 10½

Beaver Scouts
age 6 – 8

About me

My name is

✎ _____

I belong to the

✎ _____ Cub Scout Pack

All you need to know...

The Membership Award

This will be your first award in Cub Scouts. To receive it, you need to show that you understand what Cub Scouting is about. But don't panic! You will find everything you need to know here.

About my Pack

Your Pack may be part of a Scout Group. Your Group will probably also have a Beaver Scout Colony and a Scout Troop.

My Pack meets at

_____

on

_____

Colour this scarf in your Pack's colours

About your Leader

Your Leader might be called Akela. You might also call your other Leaders by names from *The Jungle Book*. Of course your Pack may use other names.

My Leader's name is

My Leader's phone number is

In my Pack, my other Leaders are called

What is The Jungle Book?

The Jungle Book is a story by Rudyard Kipling explaining how Mowgli the boy-cub joined the wolf pack.

All you need to know...

What is a Six?

You and your friends will spend time together in a team called a Six. An older Cub Scout, called a Sixer, leads each Six. A Sixer is a bit like a team captain.

My Six

I am in the

_____ Six

My Sixer's name is

_____

There are

_____ other Sixes in our Pack

My friend is

_____ who is in _____ Six

About me

My name is

_____

My birthday is on the

_____

There are

_____ people in my family

My school is

_____

My favourite TV programme is

_____

I enjoy playing / doing / going to

_____

Here is a picture of me with my Six...

All you need to know...

Traditions and ceremonies

Your Pack will have some traditions and ceremonies. Some will be used by all Cub Scout Packs. Others might be special to your Pack.

What are traditions?

Traditions are things that have been done by people for a long time.

Here are some traditions:

→ singing Happy Birthday

→ shaking hands with the other team at a football match

→ non-uniform day on the last day of term.

Can you think of any more?

The Scout Motto

is...
Be prepared

You should
'be prepared...
to have fun
to help other people
to make new friends
to do your best'

The Scout handshake

Cub Scouts shake with their left hand. Why is this? Well it all goes back to Lord Robert Baden-Powell who began Scouting...

When he was a soldier in Africa, he saw a large number of tribal chiefs who carried spears and shields. He noticed that it was a sign of great trust to offer your left hand when shaking hands. This was because you had to put down your shield and yet leave the other person holding a spear.

The Scout salute

The Scout salute is made with the right hand. It is used during the opening ceremony on Pack night. It is also used at other special times such as when you are presented with a badge.

The Scout sign

When you make your Promise you will use a special kind of salute. This is called the Scout sign. It is the same as the salute but you hold your hand at shoulder height.

All you need to know...

Types of ceremonies include:

→ Olympic medal presentations, flags and anthems

→ Teams lining up at the start of the FA Cup Final

→ Religious ceremonies

→ Changing of the Guard at Buckingham Palace

Cub Scout Ceremonies

The Grand Howl

One Cub Scout ceremony is the Grand Howl. This is a special greeting that the Pack gives to the Leader at the start of a Pack meeting. It is a type of opening ceremony.

Why is this done?

It helps you to remember your Cub Scout Promise to 'Do Your Best'.

→ All the Cub Scouts in the Pack form a circle around a Leader

→ When the Leader lowers their arms, the Pack squats down and calls out 'Akela, we'll do our best'

→ Then they all stand up

→ The Sixer leading the Grand Howl shouts out the challenge 'Cubs, do your best'

→ To which the Pack salutes and shouts back 'We will do our best!'

Flagbreak

At your Pack's opening ceremony, you will all face the flag. The Sixer leading the ceremony will pull on a rope to let the flag fly freely. This is called breaking the flag. Everyone will then salute. At the end of the meeting the Sixer will lower the flag.

Why is this done?

This is a chance to think about your Cub Scout Promise. It also makes us think of the Queen and the country in which we live.

Powerpack facts

Most Cub Scouts in the world wear the World Membership Badge. All Scouts in the United Kingdom have worn the World Membership Badge since 1971.

All you need to know...

The worldwide family of Scouting

Cub Scouts are members of a family that includes most of the countries in the world. Although they might not all be called the same names or wear the same uniform, they all enjoy having fun.

Just think, there are millions and millions of Scouts in the world! That is very difficult to imagine, isn't it?

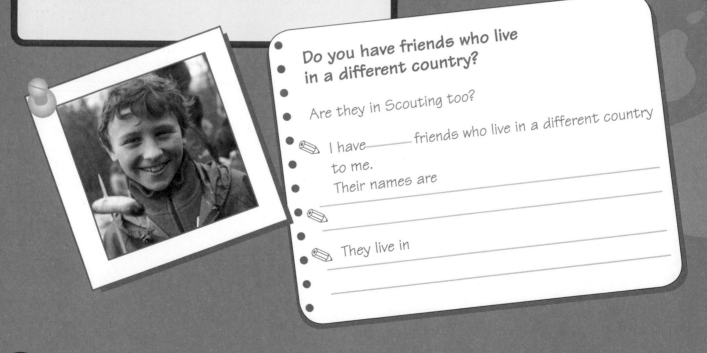

Do you have friends who live in a different country?

Are they in Scouting too?

✐ I have——— friends who live in a different country to me.
Their names are

✐

✐ They live in

Powerpack facts

Baden-Powell was the only Chief Scout of the World.

French Cub Scouts are known as Les Louvetaux.

Jamborees

Every four years, Scouts from around the world camp together at a special event called a World Jamboree. It gives them a chance to find out about each other's cultures and to make new friends.

My Investiture

The last part of your Membership Award is to make your Cub Scout Promise. You will do this at your Investiture ceremony.

What is an Investiture?

An Investiture is a special ceremony where you officially become a Cub Scout. You will gain your Membership Award and will also be presented with the World Membership Badge.

Powerpack fact

135,000 Cub Scouts meet every week in the UK. That's enough to fill the Millennium Stadium in Cardiff one and a half times!

How will I know what to do?

Before your Investiture, your Cub Scout Leader will help you practise. Your Leader will also help you to remember your Cub Scout Promise and Law.

Who will be at my Investiture?

Your Leader and fellow Cub Scouts will be there. You might also like to invite members of your family to see you make your Promise and join the Pack.

What happens at an Investiture?

The ceremony is very simple. Your Pack may have its own way of doing things, but it should go something like this:

Your Leader will ask you if you really do want to become a Cub Scout. If you do, they will ask you if you can remember the Cub Scout Law.

The Cub Scout Law

Cub Scouts always do their best

think of others before themselves

and do a good turn every day.

Then your Leader will ask you and the Pack to make the Scout sign and say the Promise. Your Leader might say a line at a time so you can repeat it.

The Promise

I promise that I will do my best
to do my duty to God
and to the Queen,
to help other people
and to keep the Cub Scout Law.

My Investiture

Here is a picture of me being invested...

My Promise

When we promise something, we are telling people that we really mean what we say. Once you understand how important a promise is, you are ready to make your Cub Scout Promise.

How can I remember my Cub Scout Promise?

We use the three fingers of the Scout sign to help us remember each part of our Cub Scout Promise:

Finger 1 – To do my duty to God

You are saying that you will try to remember:

→ to care for the world around you

→ to share the good things you have

→ to be friendly towards other people

→ to pray to God in the way you have learnt.

Finger 2 – To do my duty to the Queen

You don't have to work at a Royal Palace to serve the Queen! You can do that by obeying the laws of the land and by looking after your community. Help keep it tidy. Always try to help other people.

Finger 3 – To keep the Cub Scout Law

There are so many ways you can do this. You can:

→ really have a good go at everything that happens at Cub Scouts

→ make the most out of everything you do

→ do that little bit extra – not just enough to get by

→ do a good turn every day

→ think of all the people that you meet during the day, and think of all the small things that you could do to help them.

Badges, Awards and Challenges

You already know something about the **Membership Award** and the **World Membership Badge**. But as a Cub Scout you can earn lots of other badges too.

Joining In Badges

→ play games
→ help other people
→ share activities with other Cub Scouts

→ make things
→ be outdoors
→ try new things

For taking part in these and many other exciting activities you will get a **Joining In Badge** each year.

Activity Badges

→ If you have a special interest or hobby then you can attempt these badges.

Challenges

→ Challenges are special tasks that test your skill and determination.

The Chief Scout's Silver Award

→ This is the top award that you can achieve as a Cub Scout.

Moving-on Award

→ This badge will help you move onto the Scout Troop. In the meantime, there is plenty left to do in Cub Scouts!

Where to put your badges

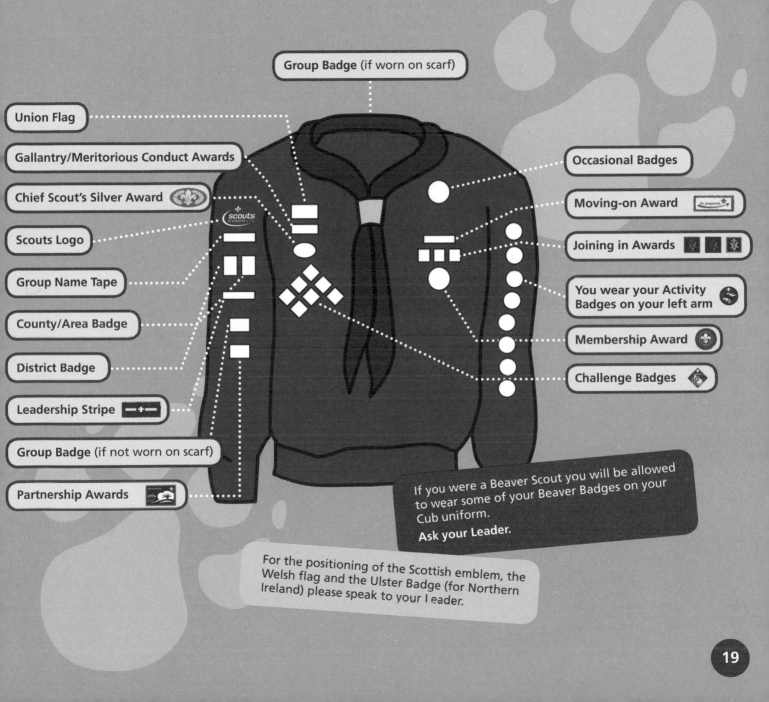

Group Badge (if worn on scarf)

Union Flag

Gallantry/Meritorious Conduct Awards

Chief Scout's Silver Award

Scouts Logo

Group Name Tape

County/Area Badge

District Badge

Leadership Stripe

Group Badge (if not worn on scarf)

Partnership Awards

Occasional Badges

Moving-on Award

Joining in Awards

You wear your Activity Badges on your left arm

Membership Award

Challenge Badges

If you were a Beaver Scout you will be allowed to wear some of your Beaver Badges on your Cub uniform.
Ask your Leader.

For the positioning of the Scottish emblem, the Welsh flag and the Ulster Badge (for Northern Ireland) please speak to your leader.

Badges

Tick the boxes as you earn each badge.

Moving-on Award

Wear the red one after moving on to the Scouts.

☐

Leadership Stripes

☐

Sixer's Stripes

☐

Seconder's Stripes

Joining In Badges

1 ☐ 2 ☐ 3 ☐ 4 ☐ 5 ☐

Membership Award

☐

Here is a picture of me wearing my uniform...

Joining In Badges

You can have lots of fun as a Cub Scout – but only if you join in!

About this badge

When you have been in the Pack for some time you will have done lots of different activities.

You will be awarded a Joining In Badge each year to show that you have taken part.

You might take part in a camp or visit a Pack meeting.

There will always be plenty of time to be with your friends, play games and try exciting new things.

How will I know what sort of things to try?

How about asking some of the Cub Scouts who already have a Joining In Badge?

Can they remember some of the things they took part in?

Here is a picture of me joining in...

Joining In...

Keep a Joining In diary

This diary will help you to remember the good times you have at Cub Scouts.

Each month, write in some of the things that you have enjoyed doing with your Pack.

Joining In diary 1st year

January

February

March

April

May

June

July

August

September

October

November

December

Joining In diary 2nd year

January

✎

February

✎

March

✎

April

✎

May

✎

June

✎

July

✎

August

✎

September

✎

October

✎

November

✎

December

✎

Joining In diary 3rd year

January

✎

February

✎

March

✎

April

✎

May

✎

June

✎

July

✎

August

✎

September

✎

October

✎

November

✎

December

✎

The Chief Scout's Silver Award

About this award

This is the top award in Cub Scouts. The Chief Scout's Silver Award shows that you have taken part in lots of interesting and exciting things with other Cub Scouts in your Pack.

Chief Scout's Silver Award

In our Scouting family, Beaver Scouts, Scouts, Explorer Scouts and members of the Scout Network can also gain a Chief Scout's Award.

Beaver Scouts can try for...
The Chief Scout's Bronze Award

Cub Scouts can try for...
The Chief Scout's Silver Award

Scouts can try for...
The Chief Scout's Gold Award

Explorer Scouts and the Scout Network can try for...
The Chief Scout's Diamond, Platinum Awards and the Queen's Scout Award.

What do I need to do?

To complete the Chief Scout's Silver Award you must:

→ Gain all 6 Challenge Badges:

- Promise Challenge
- Community Challenge
- Fitness Challenge
- Creative Challenge
- Global Challenge
- Outdoor Challenge

By completing the Outdoor Challenge you will have spent a night away from home, probably at camp. You will also have learnt some new outdoor skills and taken part in adventurous activities like canoeing, archery, or abseiling. The Outdoor Plus Challenge is an extra badge you can choose to do if you have already gained your Outdoor Challenge Badge.

Can you find these words?

(Remember to look backwards, forwards and diagonally!)

→ AKELA
→ AXE
→ CAMPING
→ FIRE
→ FLYSHEET
→ GROUNDSHEET
→ KINDLING
→ KNOTS
→ PIONEERING
→ ROPE
→ SLEEPING BAG
→ STOVE
→ TENT

```
A E D B I P M D Z Q X T L E K
T W I F X A I O A S T O N K G
E C A M P I N G T P E L A A P
E A E Q W E Y F E W M A B K I
H S A I Z S Q X N H E G S I O
S F L Y S H E E T A N E R N N
D A S A R A N A U I E A M D E
N X T A K E L A P T A J A L E
U A O A F V W E F I R E E I R
O P V P F D E G A X E A P N I
R U E R N L S A B A K A O G N
G Z D A S C L A M E A G R A G
```

Challenge Badges

We already know that there are six Challenges (and the Outdoor Plus Challenge). Now, let's find out how you can get them.

Tick the boxes as you earn each section of the badge.

Promise

Promise Challenge

About this Challenge:

When you join the Cub Scouts you promise to do your best and help other people. Here is a list of things you need to do to get your Promise Challenge. Choose FOUR from the following:

- ☐ Over a period of time help another Cub during Pack activities. This could be for a new Cub's first few weeks in the Pack, or on a residential experience.

- ☐ Over a period of time carry out good turns for someone who's not in your Pack. This could be helping a relative with housework or doing some work in the local community.

- ☐ Describe an occasion that you found particularly difficult and explain how you did your best.

- ☐ Find out about someone else who has done their best. (This could be someone famous, like an athlete or someone you know).

- ☐ Take an active part in the Leadership of the Pack.

- ☐ Help to run a Pack activity or game.

- ☐ Take part in Pack forums and be a role model for younger Cubs.

- ☐ Take an active part in an act of worship, reflection or celebration with other Cub Scouts. (This could be in the form of St George's Day celebrations, Remembrance Day or Scout's own).

- ☐ Find out about a faith other than your own. This should include places of worship and a festival or ceremony. If possible a visit to a place of worship should be undertaken or a visit from a religious leader arranged.

- ☐ Gain the My Faith Activity Badge.

What's a Challenge?

A challenge is a special task that will test your skill and determination.

Community

Community Challenge

About this Challenge:

Helping out in your community is a very important part of being a Cub Scout. For this Challenge you need to complete THREE of the following:

☐ Find out about a place of worship (preferably different from your own) in your local community. Find out what happens there and tell other Cub Scouts about it. If possible, visit a place of worship or meet a religious leader.

☐ Organise a fundraising event for a charity of your choice.

☐ Over a period of a month take good care of a pet. Make a record of how you have cared for your pet, for example, food, exercise, and cleaning/grooming.

☐ Meet or visit someone who helps their local community, for example, a Police officer, a Fire fighter or Lifeboat crew member. Explain to others what you have learned and how we can help them to do their job.

☐ Find out what possible dangers there could be in your home, Meeting Place or on a campsite. Help other Cub Scouts to be aware of any dangers.

☐ Learn basic First Aid — control bleeding, burns and scalds, airway protection and how and when to get help.

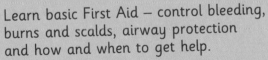

Powerpack fact

A Sikh temple is called a Gurdwara.

Fitness

Fitness Challenge

About this Challenge:

This gives you a chance to find out how fit you are. Your Fitness Challenge is about improving your fitness over a number of weeks.

What you need to do:

- [ ] Show how you have done your best in a sport or activity over a two-week period. This can be something new or a sport/activity you currently take part in.

- [ ] Show how you have improved your physical fitness over a two-week period. You could examine what you eat and improve your diet, how much exercise you take, how much sleep you get. Explain how you might continue to improve your fitness in the future

- [ ] Try two new sports or physical activities at least once. This could include tennis, dance, basketball or Tai Chi.

Creative Challenge

About this Challenge:

Getting creative is one of the fun things to do when you are a Cub Scout. You can sing, make things, take photographs – lots of different activities. To get your Creative Challenge Badge you need to complete THREE of the following:

☐ Create and then read or perform a prayer, reading or sketch for a service, about your Promise. This should include why your Promise is important to you or how you have used your Promise to help other people. This could be done on your own or in a small group.

☐ Plan and perform a musical performance, play or sketch.

☐ Create two new games for the Pack.

☐ Design and make something, for example, a birdhouse, model or kite.

☐ Create something using information technology, for example, a birthday card, party invitation, or a poster.

☐ Make a creative presentation about one thing about Cub Scouting. You could make a video, photos or posters. It could show the activities you enjoy doing, a Cub camp or be used for encouraging other young people to join Cubs.

☐ Write a poem or short story on a subject of your choice.

☐ Design and make something using pioneering skills. This could be a raft or a scaled down model of a bridge.

☐ Take part in an activity where you have to solve a problem. This could be an incident hike or a code breaking activity at camp.

Powerpack fact

You don't just need pencils and crayons to get creative. A computer is a great way to design a poster.

31

Global Challenge

About this Challenge:

Knowing about the world, its different people, countries and traditions is an exciting part of being a Cub Scout. When you are a Scout you may be lucky enough to go to a Jamboree. A Jamboree is where lots of Scouts from many different countries camp together. Here is a list of things you need to do to complete the Global Challenge.

Complete FOUR of the following:

- ☐ Find out about the traditions, culture, food, religion and other interesting things of a country different from your own.

- ☐ Find out about the work of an international charity that helps around the world, such as OXFAM or UNICEF. Present your findings to the rest of the Pack

- ☐ Find something out about international Scouting. You could take part in a 'Join In Jamboree' activity, or arrange a visit from a Jamboree participant. Or, you could find out about Scouting in a country of your choice

- ☐ Find out about things that can be recycled or how energy can be saved. Over a period of weeks, show how you have recycled or saved energy at home.

- ☐ Find out about a global issue such as poverty, conservation or water and sanitation and what you can do to help

- ☐ Find out about a technology of your choice. This could be a personal computer, a car engine or even an aircraft. You should understand the basic functions of the technology and how it is used. You should also find out about its history. Present your findings to the rest of the Pack.

Outdoor Challenge

About this Challenge:

Being out in the open is an important part of being a Cub Scout. Here is a list of things you need to do to complete your Outdoor Challenge.

- ☐ Take part in at least one residential experience (preferably camping) with a minimum of two nights away. You don't have to camp two nights in a row

- ☐ Explain to other Cub Scouts what activity you enjoyed most whilst on the residential experience and what activity you found hardest. You could make a poster, tell a story, or perhaps take some photographs and show them to the Pack

- ☐ Learn two new skills and use them, for example: tracking, fire lighting or some basic knots

- ☐ Take part in three new outdoor activities that you have not done before, for example, shelter building, pioneering, archery, skiing, abseiling, a wide game or kite flying.

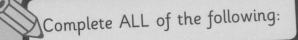

Outdoor Plus Challenge

About this Challenge:

The Outdoor Plus Challenge is an extra challenge. Before you start you need to hold the Outdoor Challenge.

☐ Take an active part in helping to plan or run the night's away experience; for example help a less experienced Cub Scout during the event or plan and lead a Scouts' Own or game.

☐ Know how to prepare for a one-day expedition to the countryside (e.g. correct clothing, footwear, First Aid kit and food and drink).

☐ Spend two nights away with other Cub Scouts (as well as the nights away used for the Outdoor Challenge. They do not have be two nights in a row).

☐ Plan and then travel along a route of at least one kilometre on foot, bicycle, skateboard or similar. Navigate using any of the following:

Compass
Map
Landmarks
Tracking signs
Taped instructions

☐ Or plan and then use a route using at least two types of public transport. The route should not be one that is familiar to you.

Powerpack fact

Scouts are world-class tent-pitchers. They won the World Tent-pitching Championship in 2006.

More about Challenges...

Can I attempt these Challenges more than once?

Yes, but if you do, then the second time you should try to help younger members of the Pack with their Challenges.

When you have completed a Challenge, colour in one of the balls.

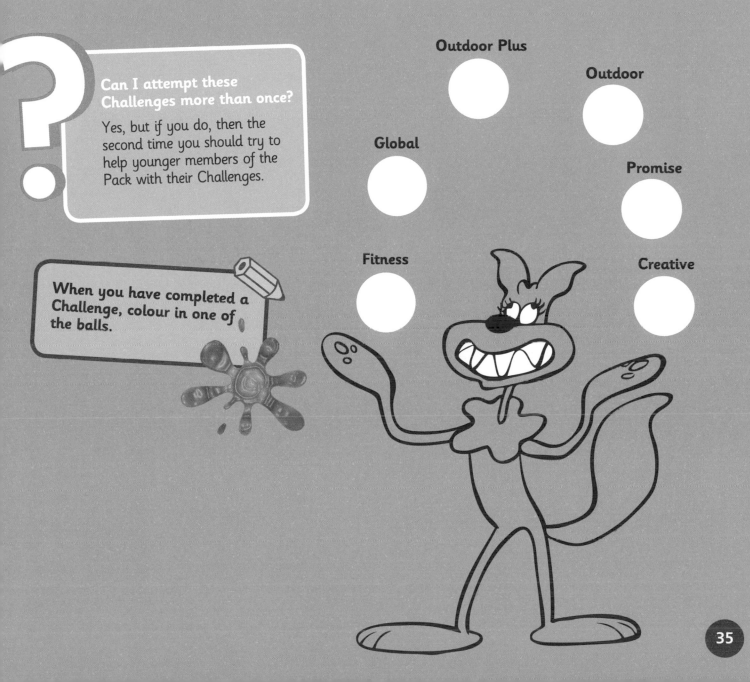

Outdoor Plus

Outdoor

Global

Promise

Fitness

Creative

Partnership Awards

Partnership Awards let you try new and exciting Scouting activities.

You can do Partnership Awards with people of different ages in your Scout Group or with groups outside Scouting.

Work together with other Sections, and the members of your Group's Beaver Scout Colony, Scout Troop or Explorer Scout Unit to get these Awards.

Tick the boxes as you earn each badge.

International Friendship Partnership Award

☐ Find out about how people live in different countries. Why not try and meet some Scouts from another country?

International

Powerpack fact

There are Scouts in 216 different countries and territories in the world.

Faith Partnership Award

Faith

☐ In your Pack, learn about other faiths in your area. You could invite a Cub Pack from a different faith group to your meeting, such as a Muslim or Sikh Group.

Environment Partnership Award

☐ Find out about the environment and what you can do to help look after it.

Environment

Activity Badges

One of the best things about being a Cub Scout is doing lots of exciting activities and gaining badges. There are 33 badges to choose from. As you go through and complete each section of a badge, tick them off so you can see how you are doing.

Some of the wording has been simplified. Visit www.scouts.org.uk for the original list. Speak to your Leader if there's an Activity Badge you would like to do.

Tick the boxes as you earn each section of the badge.

Air Activities

☐ Know the dangers of visiting an airfield

☐ Visit an airfield, air display or air museum

Choose THREE things from the list below:

☐ Make and fly one of these: a model aeroplane, three different types of paper glider, a hot-air balloon, or a kite

☐ Identify six airlines from their markings

☐ Name and identify the main parts of an aeroplane

☐ Make a plastic scale model aeroplane

☐ Name and identify the different types of aircraft. This could be aeroplanes, airships, gliders or even hot air balloons

☐ Fly in an aircraft and tell your Pack about it

☐ Explain to your Pack how different weather conditions can affect air activities

☐ Collect and identify six different pictures of aircraft and share them with other Cub Scouts.

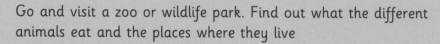

Powerpack web

These people can give you more information or help you with this badge:
RSPB – visit www.rspb.org.uk/youth

Pets at Home run free pet care workshops at local stores visit www.petsathome.com

Complete THREE of the following:

Animal Carer

☐ Go and visit a zoo or wildlife park. Find out what the different animals eat and the places where they live

☐ Look after a pet for three months and know the right foods to give it. Know how to recognise illnesses that many animals get and how to make them better

☐ Help to look after a farm animal and know the right food to give it. Know how to recognise illnesses that many farm animals get. Find out what special care is needed before and after the birth of farm animals

☐ Keep a record of birds, animal and/or insect life in your garden or local area/park. You can use pictures, sketches, photographs or tape recordings

☐ Know about six different freshwater, seawater or tropical fish, and then find out what kinds of food they eat

☐ Join an animal, bird or wildlife society. Take part in its activities, or try one of their awards or badges

☐ Find out about dangers to wildlife in the countryside. Then, make a poster, collage or drawing or tell other Cub Scouts what you found out.

Artist

Complete THREE activities from the list below. One of them should be done when a Leader is with you.

- [ ] Draw with pencil, brush, pen or crayon a picture of any imaginary incident, character or scene
- [ ] Design and make a greetings card
- [ ] Make a poster advertising Cub Scouting or a Cub Scout event
- [ ] Make a design and print it on paper or fabric. You could use potato or lino cuts
- [ ] Design and make a decorated book cover
- [ ] Draw or paint a picture from still life or a landscape
- [ ] Make a display of photographs on a subject that interests you
- [ ] Make a video on a subject that interests you
- [ ] Design and build a model
- [ ] Visit an art gallery
- [ ] Make a model out of clay.

Astronomer

Complete ALL of the following:

- [ ] Make a model or draw a simple diagram of the solar system
- [ ] Explain the difference between a planet and a star
- [ ] Identify three constellations
- [ ] Find out about and present some information on two of the following: planets, comets, the Northern Lights, the sun, eclipses, meteorites, black holes, the moon, light years, space exploration or any other space related subject
- [ ] Look at the moon, using binoculars or a telescope if you can. Describe some of its features
- [ ] Know how to find and recognise the pole star or southern star. Know how explorers used it to find out which way to go.

Athletics

☐ Take part in an appropriate warm-up and warm-down routine, lead by a suitable person (e.g. adult, Young Leader or Scout), using all the main muscle groups. For example: skipping, running on the spot, stretching both arms high above the head and then relaxing down, bending the knees and dropping the head, rolling the head slowly around tensing and relaxing the shoulders

☐ Explain the most appropriate clothing to wear and how to be safe when taking part in athletic activities.

☐ Take part in one of the throwing activities:
• Throw a tennis or cricket ball both over arm and under arm, as far you can
• Throw three bean bags into a bucket increasing the distance each time
• Throw a football sized ball, using a chest push and overhead throw, as far as you can

☐ Take part in two of the following running activities, trying your best:
• Shuttle run 6 x 10m
• 50m skip with a rope
• 50m sprint
• 25m sack race
• 25m egg and spoon race
• 400m run

☐ Take part in one of the following team activities:
• 4 x 100m relay
• Team assault course
• Assisted blindfold race

☐ Take part in one of the following jumps, going as far or as high as you can:
• Sargent jump
• Standing jump
• High jump
• Long jump

Notes

• This badge is awarded for participation and putting in your best effort.

• For the high jump, special attention must be given to the nature of the jump, and the landing facilities required.

Unless expert tuition and supervision is available, you must not attempt the Fosbury Flop.

• The badge could be gained by taking part in a sports day in the Pack or in the District which includes these activities

Athletics plus

☐ Hold the Athletics Activity Badge

☐ Gain eight or more points by adding together the scores from the best four events from the table below:

Events	3 points	2 points	1 point
50m sprint	☐ 9 seconds	☐ 10 seconds	☐ 11 seconds
Throwing a cricket ball	☐ 25 metres	☐ 22 metres	☐ 18 metres
High jump	☐ 96 cm	☐ 86 cm	☐ 76 cm
Long jump	☐ 3 metres	☐ 2.5 metres	☐ 2 metres
Sargent jump	☐ 35 cm	☐ 30 cm	☐ 25 cm
Shuttle run 6x10 metres	☐ 18 seconds	☐ 19 seconds	☐ 20 seconds
50m skip with a rope	☐ 12 seconds	☐ 13 seconds	☐ 14 seconds
1,000m run	☐ 5 minutes	☐ 6 minutes	☐ 10 minutes

Notes

- For the high jump, special attention must be given to the nature of the jump, and the landing facilities required. Unless expert tuition and supervision is available, you must not attempt the Fosbury Flop.

- For the sargent jump, the measurements refer to the height of the target when held at full arm's stretch by the participants.

- For the shuttle run, the limits are marked on the ground. Your hand or foot must touch on or past the mark at the end of the run.

Complete ALL activities from the list below

Book Reader

- [ ] Make a list of at least six books you have read or used recently. Name the authors. Tell your Leader or other members of your Pack about three of the books. Your three books should have at least one fiction (story) and one non-fiction (non-story) book

- [ ] Understand and know how to care for your books

- [ ] Show that you know how to use a dictionary, encyclopaedia and an atlas

- [ ] Explain to a Leader how the books in a library are set out and how you would find fiction and non-fiction books.

Camper

Complete ALL of the following:

- [ ] With other Cub Scouts, camp under canvas for at least three nights (they don't have to be on the same camp)

- [ ] Help pack your personal kit for a Cub Scout camp

- [ ] Help to pitch and strike a tent and know how to take care of it

- [ ] At camp, help to prepare, cook, serve and clear away a simple meal. Do this outside

- [ ] Know how to look after yourself and be safe at camp. Know how to get ready for tent and kit inspection

Take part in at least THREE of these while at camp:

- [ ] Campfire

- [ ] Scouts' Own

- [ ] Wide game

- [ ] Joint activity with other Cub Scouts on site or from a local Group

- [ ] A good turn for the site

- [ ] Help to tidy up the campsite before you leave.

Chef

Complete ALL of the following:

- [ ] Know the basic rules of safety and hygiene in the kitchen and why they are important
- [ ] Talk with your Leader about the different ways of preparing and cooking food. Think about what is good and bad about each one
- [ ] Talk about the importance of a balanced diet
- [ ] When a Leader is with you, plan, cook, serve and clear away a two-course meal for at least two people. Talk about your menu with the people you are cooking for. You need to prepare and cook vegetables in the meal
- [ ] Make scones, small cakes, biscuits or tarts.

➝

You could make these as part of your menu:

Main courses
Shepherd's pie, curry and rice ham salad vegetable lasagne

Desserts
Fruit crumble
Fresh fruit salad

Collector

Complete ALL of the following:

- [ ] Make a collection of similar items for three months. Choose something you enjoy, such as: stamps, coins, postcards or fossils
- [ ] Display your collection in an exciting and interesting way
- [ ] Talk about things in your collection that particularly interest you
- [ ] Look at a collection made by someone else. Say what you like and don't like about the collection.

Communicator

Complete ALL of the following:

- [ ] Show that you can use a public telephone
- [ ] Describe how to make an emergency call, and what you would need to tell the emergency operator
- [ ] Receive directions or instructions to do something. Check with the person who gives the information that you have understood and then follow the directions or instructions
- [ ] Ask someone you know to give you a call. Write down the message, making sure you record everything important
- [ ] Find out how to use three of the following things:

  1. Mobile phone, email, text messages, pager or voice mail, answering machine, fax machine. 2. Show a Leader you can use them.

Do THREE of the following:

- [ ] Make a spoken, taped or a newsletter report of a local event either past or present
- [ ] Make and keep a link with another Cub Scout Pack using tapes, videos, letters, email etc. for an agreed time
- [ ] Find out how people with visual or hearing difficulties communicate (e.g. Braille, Makaton or British Sign Language). Learn a simple phrase in another type of communication like these
- [ ] Tell a story about an experience you have had with your Leaders and other Cub Scouts. Make sure that you communicate clearly and that those listening can understand the story
- [ ] Have a simple conversation in another language
- [ ] Write three simple messages using codes, ciphers, invisible ink, or semaphore, then write them in English
- [ ] Memorise a short message and re-tell it 15 minutes later
- [ ] Pass a message to someone using amateur radio.

Some of the wording has been simplified. Visit www.scouts.org.uk for the original list. Speak to your Leader if there's an Activity Badge you would like to do.

44

Cyclist

Complete ALL of the following:

- ☐ Own or have regular use of a bicycle of a suitable size and a cycle helmet.
- ☐ Be able to clean and oil a bicycle. Show how to pump up the tyres and how to mend a puncture.
- ☐ Understand the need for keeping a bicycle locked when leaving it unattended.
- ☐ Make a poster to promote road safety to pedestrians or cyclists.
- ☐ Discuss with your leader or other Cub Scouts the safety measures necessary for riding in poor conditions.

Do ONE of these:

- ☐ Be able to mount and dismount properly.
- ☐ Understand the need for keeping the bicycle in a roadworthy condition, and how to do this.
- ☐ Understand the need for lights and reflective clothing.
- ☐ Under observation, in a safe place, go for a short ride to show that you can ride safely and confidently

Or: gain Bikeability Level 2 or 3

Notes
Cycle helmets should be worn at all times during cycling activities.

DIY

Complete ALL of the following:

- ☐ Show how to use safely, and how to take care of, tools such as a hammer, a saw, a screwdriver, spanners, pliers, a hand-drill, a glue gun etc.
- ☐ Show how to prepare and paint a vertical surface with paintbrushes, roller or pad and show how to clean them.

Help design and make TWO items from the following:

- ☐ A nesting box or window box
- ☐ A box for storing tools, pencils, tapes
- ☐ A rack for keys, mugs or coats
- ☐ Book-ends or bookstand
- ☐ A shoe rack
- ☐ Noticeboard for camp
- ☐ Letter holder
- ☐ Towel rail.

Entertainer

Complete TWO of the following:

☐ Help to make up a mime or play and perform it

☐ Perform a puppet play or shadowgraph using puppets, which you have made

☐ Help to plan and make an entertainment recorded on video or audiotape

☐ Sing two songs

☐ Perform folk or traditional dances

☐ Make a selection of simple rhythm instruments and use them as accompaniments

☐ Tell a story to an audience

☐ Make up and perform a dance to a piece of music of your choice

☐ Help plan and perform a series of magic tricks

☐ Take part in a show, concert or band performance.

Equestrian

Complete ALL of the following:

☐ Show how to get on and off a horse safely

☐ Show the correct position in the saddle

☐ Show how to hold the reins correctly

☐ Show how to ride safely in an enclosed area without a leading rein. This should include walking and trotting

Show TWO of the following skills:

☐ Walking without stirrups

☐ Walking on a loose rein and shortening the reins

☐ Cantering

☐ Riding up and down a hill at walking pace

☐ Riding over a single pole or very small fence.

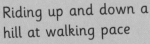

Global Conservation

You must carry out these projects as a member of a group of Cub Scouts and not alone. This group can be your Six or another small group

While you are working on this badge with your group:

 Find some examples showing how people have damaged the environment and other examples showing how people have conserved the environment

☐ Find examples of where the Countryside Code is being broken and what has happened as a result

☐ Take part as a group in two projects, such as:

- Clearing a ditch, pond or creek

- Making, setting up and maintaining a bird feeder, bird table, bird nesting box or bird bath

- Looking after a piece of land or a garden

- Tidying up a piece of wasteland

- Taking part in an anti-litter campaign

- Planting a tree or shrub

- Looking after a compost bin.

Complete ONE of the following:

☐ Make a display to tell others about an animal, bird, plant, fish etc, which is in danger of extinction

☐ Organise a 'save it' campaign to encourage others to conserve energy, e.g. home insulation, fuel efficient engines, etc.

☐ Take part in or start a recycling scheme, e.g. bottles, cans, waste paper

☐ Visit a forest, wood or campsite and take part in a project on tree conservation. With expert help, find out how trees can be cared for.

Hobbies

Write your hobby below

_____

Complete ALL of the following:

- [ ] Know any safety rules for your hobby
- [ ] Show a continuing interest in your chosen hobby, interest or activity for two months
- [ ] Show your Leader, or other Cub Scouts, how you pursue your hobby, interest or activity. Show what equipment, materials and background information you have used
- [ ] Talk with your Leader about how you plan to develop your hobby, interest or skill in the future.

Powerpack fact

You can do more than one Hobbies Badge!

Some of the wording has been simplified. Visit www.scouts.org.uk for the original list. Speak to your Leader if there's an Activity Badge you would like to do.

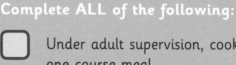

Home Help

Complete ALL of the following:

- [ ] Under adult supervision, cook a simple one course meal
- [ ] Lay a table and serve a simple meal. This can be done with requirement number one
- [ ] Wash up afterwards and show how to clean a saucepan or similar cooking utensils, cutlery, glassware, etc. This may include loading and unloading a dishwasher
- [ ] Under adult supervision, wash and iron your Group Scarf
- [ ] Sew on a badge or button
- [ ] Keep your room clean and tidy and make your bed for a week
- [ ] Clean two of the following: windows, silver, brass-work, basin or cupboard
- [ ] Clean and tidy a living room.

Home Safety

Complete ALL of the following:

- [ ] Know what to do if you have a burst water pipe, gas leak or electricity power failure at home
- [ ] Know how to protect your home from fire. Know what to do if a fire starts at your home
- [ ] Know what makes many accidents at home happen and how they can be prevented
- [ ] Know what to do to protect your house from crime
- [ ] Know how to make an emergency telephone call, including using mobile telephones, to call the emergency services. Know where the nearest public telephone box is to your house, or where you can make an emergency call should your phone be broken
- [ ] Make a list of useful emergency numbers.

Local Knowledge

Complete THREE of the following:

Either:

- [ ] Find out about someone who lived in or near where you live who was or is famous

Or:

- [ ] Visit and find out about a famous old building, monument, earthworks or other place of historical interest. Talk about what you have found out with your Leader or other Cub Scouts
- [ ] Find out the meaning of, and collect pictures of, either your County, Borough, District, town or village coat of arms. Tell your Leader in how many different places you have seen the coat of arms displayed
- [ ] Talk to someone who has lived in your local area for a long time. Find out about what they did when they were young and what changes they have seen in your local area over the past years
- [ ] Draw a map of your area and mark on it places of interest
- [ ] With other Cub Scouts, go on a short walk in your local area. Point out to your Leader(s) anything you find interesting
- [ ] Visit a local emergency service station such as police, fire, ambulance services, coastguard or mountain rescue. Find out how the station is run.

Map Reader

Complete ALL of the following:

- [ ] Know how to use the key of an Ordnance Survey map
- [ ] Be able to use six figure grid references
- [ ] Explain how to find north on a map and how to set a map to north
- [ ] Locate your home and Pack Meeting Place on an Ordnance Survey or street map
- [ ] Understand contour lines on an Ordnance Survey map
- [ ] Be able to identify 10 Ordnance Survey map symbols
- [ ] Use an Ordnance Survey map during an outdoor activity
- [ ] Know the eight points of a compass and use them during an outdoor activity.

Martial Arts

Complete ALL of the following:

- [ ] Take part in a martial art activity (recognised by the Sports Council) regularly and show improvement
- [ ] Talk with your Leader about the skills you need and what the rules are
- [ ] Take part in an exhibition or competition.

Powerpack fact

There are lots of different kinds of maps: Geological, Political and Social.

My Faith

Find out about your place of worship including something about each of the following:

- ☐ The people involved, their titles and what they do
- ☐ The important or sacred objects
- ☐ The festivals and customs
- ☐ The stories and traditions. These could be from books, videos or other sources
- ☐ Choose a favourite religious song or hymn and sing it with other Cub Scouts. You should explain to the Pack why you like it and what it means to you
- ☐ Choose a favourite prayer or reading and share it with the Pack at an appropriate occasion (you may write the prayer and should explain to the Pack why you like it and what it means to you).

Naturalist

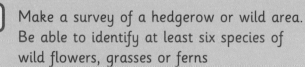

Complete THREE of the following:

- ☐ Make a survey of a hedgerow or wild area. Be able to identify at least six species of wild flowers, grasses or ferns
- ☐ Keep a record of birds you have spotted over one week. Be able to identify at least six wild birds
- ☐ Make a survey of a pond, river, stream or seashore. Be able to identify some of the animals, fish, insects or plant life you find

- ☐ Be able to identify six types of insect you find
- ☐ Identify six different trees or shrubs from their leaves, shape, fruit or nuts and make a bark rubbing
- ☐ Identify six butterflies, moths or frogs and talk to a Leader about their life cycle.

Navigator

With other Cub Scouts, go for a walk with a Leader around the local area. Take it in turns to use one or more of the following types of navigation:

- Written instructions
- Taped instructions
- Road signs
- Tracking signs
- Maps
- By drawing a simple map, direct someone from your Meeting Place to a local railway station, bus stop, hospital, doctor, post office, etc.
- Using a local street map, find certain roads and places of interest as requested by your Leader
- Help plan, or take part in, a treasure hunt using clues, directions and signs to reach an unknown destination.

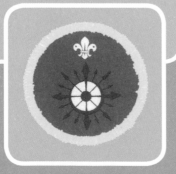

Personal Safety

Complete ALL of the following:

- Explain the dangers of playing on or visiting near two of the following: railways, busy roads, building sites, cliffs, canal banks, sand/gravel pits, farmyards, river banks, quarries, moorlands and lakes
- Take part in a fire drill. Know what to do to help protect your home, Meeting Place, Pack camp and Pack holiday against the risk of fire. Explain the importance of a working smoke detector. Know what you would do in the event of a fire in your home
- Show you can use at least one of the following codes: Green Cross Code, Water Safety Code, Bathing Code, Firework Code etc. Make up a safety code of your own choice, e.g. car passenger, train passenger, or the playground
- Know how to use a public telephone and how to make an emergency phone call, including using a mobile telephone
- Explain what you must do if a stranger starts to talk to you and what you must tell your parents/carers, if you are going out without them
- Know how and why you might contact helplines such as Childline
- Explain the best way to stay safe while online. Write some common sense rules to observe while you are on the Internet.

Physical Recreation

Complete ALL of the following:

- [ ] Show a good sporting attitude in all games and sports in which you take part
- [ ] Tell a Leader about the sports you take part in. Find out as much as you can about the sports, especially the rules
- [ ] Show reasonable skill and take part regularly in at least one of your chosen sports
  - [ ] Bring along the clothing and equipment for the sport selected above and show how to look after it
  - [ ] Tell a Leader what training and preparation you do for your chosen sport and how and when you practise.

Road Safety

Complete ALL of the following:

- [ ] Draw or photograph 10 different traffic signs and explain what they mean
- [ ] Show how to use the Green Cross Code
- [ ] Tell a Leader about why different types of pedestrian crossing are important and know how to use them safely
- [ ] Show that you know how to behave safely as a car passenger
- [ ] Show how to use a public telephone or mobile telephone and know how to make an emergency telephone call
- [ ] Make a poster to promote road safety to pedestrians or cyclists.

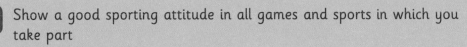

GREEN CROSS CODE:

STOP
LOOK
LISTEN!

Complete SIX activities, three from Part A and three from Part B. For each, explain or show to a Leader what has been done and the conclusions made.

Scientist

Part A: The Physical World

☐ Make a simple switch. Show how it could be used to control a light bulb powered by a battery.

☐ Show how electrical currents produce magnetic, chemical and heating effects, and explain what happens

☐ Show that hot air rises

☐ Make an artificial rainbow by splitting up a beam of white light

☐ Make a pin-hole camera and understand how it works

☐ Keep simple weather records over a month, e.g. rainfall, temperature, cloud cover, wind direction

☐ Make a simple compass and show the effects of metallic and magnetic materials upon it

☐ Make a simple periscope

☐ Show how to recover dissolved substances from a water solution

☐ Recognise three different constellations

☐ Make a model to show how the earth orbits the sun.

Some of the wording has been simplified. Visit www.scouts.org.uk for the original list. Speak to your Leader if there's an Activity Badge you would like to do.

Part B: The Living World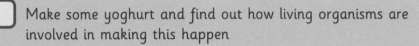

- ☐ Make some yoghurt and find out how living organisms are involved in making this happen

- ☐ Grow cress (or a similar plant) and investigate what happens when light and water are excluded from it

- ☐ Use a net and jar to find out how many different creatures live in the water and mud at the edge of a pond

- ☐ Set up a wormery or ant colony and record the activity over a few weeks

- ☐ Grow a bean or pea. When the root and shoot are visible investigate what happens when the seed is turned upside down and left to continue growing

- ☐ Collect seeds from various plants and discover how these are protected and dispersed

- ☐ Grow crystals or make crystal shapes from paper

- ☐ Investigate what happens to your pulse rate before, during and after exercise.

Skater

Complete ALL of the following:

 Own, or have used, in-line, quad or ice skates, or a skateboard for at least three months

 Know some safety rules about skating on a road and in other public places. Show what clothing and protective equipment (helmet, knee pads, elbow pads etc.) you should wear for the chosen activity

☐ Show how to start, stop and turn safely

☐ Show how to fall safely and regain balance.

Sports Enthusiast

Complete ALL of the following:

☐ Learn the rules and laws for a sport, then explain them to an adult

☐ Know about the teams and people who do your chosen sport

☐ Explain what equipment people need to do the sport

☐ List some major events that happen in your sport

☐ Tell your Leader about the times you have gone to watch events for your sport. If you haven't been, explain how you keep up to date with your sport.

Water Activities

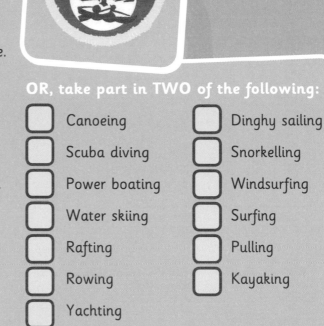

- [ ] Explain the safety rules that apply to all water activities.

Either complete one of the following:

- [ ] Complete two sessions of canoeing and gain the British Canoe Union's Paddlepower Start Certificate.
- [ ] Qualify for the Royal Yachting Association Young Sailing Scheme - Start Sailing Stage 1.
- [ ] Qualify for the British Sub Aqua Club's Basic Snorkel Diver Qualification.
- [ ] Qualify for the Professional Association of Diving Instructors' Discover Scuba (Bubble Maker), or Seal Team Programme.
- [ ] Qualify for the British Surfing Association's Junior Scheme Level One Award.
- [ ] Qualify for the British Water Ski & Wakeboard – Cutting Edge participation certificate

OR, take part in TWO of the following:

- [ ] Canoeing
- [ ] Scuba diving
- [ ] Power boating
- [ ] Water skiing
- [ ] Rafting
- [ ] Rowing
- [ ] Yachting
- [ ] Dinghy sailing
- [ ] Snorkelling
- [ ] Windsurfing
- [ ] Surfing
- [ ] Pulling
- [ ] Kayaking

World Faiths

Complete ALL of the following:

- [ ] Visit a place of worship you have never been to before and find out some information about the building, its contents and its form of worship
- [ ] Meet someone who belongs to a faith or denomination other than your own. Find out how they practise their faith
- [ ] Find out about the holy places associated with a faith other than your own
- [ ] Find out about the religious festivals and customs for a faith other than your own.

Staged Activity Badges

There are six Staged Activity Badges you can attempt. Each badge has five or more stages. It is your level of skill and not how old you are that is important.

You can find the full requirements of all six Staged Activity Badges at www.scouts.org.uk/cubs

Emergency Aid

Hikes Away

IT

Nights Away

Musician

Swimmer.

Tick each box as you complete each stage.

Emergency Aid
Stage 1
Complete ALL the following:

- ☐ Understand and recognise dangers in the house and outside
- ☐ Know what to do at the scene of an accident
- ☐ Know how to open an airway
- ☐ Know how to treat minor cuts, scratches and grazes.

Powerpack fact
The Staged Activity Badges go on the left arm of your uniform

Some of the wording has been simplified. Visit www.scouts.org.uk for the original list. Speak to your Leader if there's an Activity Badge you would like to do.

Stage 2

Complete ALL of the following:

- [ ] Know what to do at the scene of an accident
- [ ] Know how to get help from the emergency service
- [ ] Know how to clear an airway and place in the recovery position
- [ ] Know how to deal with minor bleeding
- [ ] Know how to deal with major bleeding
- [ ] Know how to deal with burns and scalds.

Stage 3

Complete ALL of the following:

- [ ] Know what to do at the scene of an accident
- [ ] Know when and how to contact the Emergency Services
- [ ] Be able to respond to the needs of an unconscious patient. Know how to open an airway, give CPR and how to place in the recovery position
- [ ] Know how to deal with major bleeding
- [ ] Know how to deal with burns and scalds
- [ ] Know how to safeguard against the effects of heat. Know how to recognise and treat heat exhaustion
- [ ] Know how to safeguard against the effects of cold. Know how to recognise and treat hypothermia
- [ ] Recognise if someone is in shock and how to treat them
- [ ] Know how to deal with choking.

Powerpack fact

When you are called on to help someone with your Emergency Aid training remember:
- never put yourself in danger
- don't be shy — ask an adult for help
- if you have any doubt, call an ambulance.

59

Hikes Away

- [ ] Complete one hike or journey. Talk with your Leader first and agree where you will go, and why. You must have the right clothes and equipment for the conditions and the terrain.

Each hike should last about three hours. Examples might be:

- [ ] Follow a towpath trail and discover how locks work on the local canal

- [ ] While on camp or pack holiday explore on foot a local town or village

- [ ] Walk up a hill and enjoy the view.

Make a note of the number of hikes away you do. This could be up to 50!

- [ ] 5 Hikes Away
- [ ] 10 Hikes Away
- [ ] 20 Hikes Away
- [ ] 35 Hikes Away
- [ ] 50 Hikes Away.

Information Technology 1

Complete ALL of the following:

- [ ] Show that you can switch on and close down a computer safely

- [ ] Show that you know what the following are:
  Monitor
  Mouse
  Printer
  CD-ROM
  Icon

- [ ] Use a piece of software of your choice to show that you can produce a poster to show others what you do in Scouting. Use text and graphics

- [ ] Use a piece of painting software to produce a simple picture

- [ ] Show you can use a piece of software that requires the use of a CD-ROM.

Information Technology 2

Complete ALL of the following:

- [ ] Produce a list of rules for using the Internet safely

- [ ] Show that you know what the following terms mean:
  Modem
  Browser
  Search engine
  Digital camera
  Clip art
  Scanner
  Menu

- [ ] Show that you can save a file and open that file at a later date.

Choose FOUR of these activities to complete:

- [ ] Access the Internet safely, to find out as much as you can about a topic of your choice

- [ ] Use a digital camera to take some digital photographs and use a piece of software to enhance or alter the original photographs

- [ ] Use a piece of software of your choice to produce a set of matching stationery for an event. It could be for a birthday and you make the place name cards, invitations and even posters

- [ ] Use a piece of simulation software and explain what you learnt from it. This could be driving a car

- [ ] Produce a series of newsletters for your Section over a three-month period

- [ ] Produce a simple pictogram or graph of something of interest to you or your Section.

Musician 1

Skill

Listen to a short tune of a couple of lines and then sing it back

Listen to another tune and then beat or clap out the rhythm

Performance

Sing or play two different types of song or tune on any instrument you like. Perform it in front of other Scouts, or at a public performance, such as at a Group Show, school concert or church service.

Knowledge

Demonstrate some of the musical exercises that you use to practise your skills

Talk about your instrument and why you enjoy playing it or the songs you sing and why you enjoy singing them

Name a few popular pieces of music that can be played on your instrument

Name several musicians who you have heard. You don't have to like them!

Interest

Tell your assessor about the music that you most like to listen to.

Powerpack fact

There are lots of different musical bands you can join in Scouting. There are marching bands, concert bands, brass bands, jazz bands, and even heavy metal bands. If you think you're ready, ask your Leader if there is one near you.

Some of the wording has been simplified. Visit www.scouts.org.uk for the original list. Speak to your Leader if there's an Activity Badge you would like to do.

Musician 2

Complete ALL of the following:

☐ **Skill**

Achieve Grade One of the Associated Board of the Royal School of Music (or similar) on the instrument of your choice or by singing.

☐ **Performance**

Sing or play two different types of song or tune on your chosen instrument. Perform it in front of other Scouts, or at a public performance, such as at a Group Show, school concert or church service.

☐ **Knowledge**

Demonstrate some of the musical exercises that you use to practise your skills

Talk about your instrument and why you enjoy playing it (or the songs you sing and why you enjoy singing them)

Name several well-known pieces of music associated with your instrument

Name several musicians who are associated with your instrument or chosen songs.

☐ **Interest**

Talk about your own interests in music, including what you listen to most. How is this similar to or different from the music you play or sing.

Musician 3

Complete ALL of the following:

☐ **Skill**

Achieve Grade Two of the Associated Board of the Royal School of Music (or similar) on the instrument of your choice.

☐ **Performance**

Sing or play (either as a solo or with others) two different types of song or tune on your chosen instrument. This performance must be either in front of the other Scouts, or at a public performance such as at a Group Show, school concert or church service.

☐ **Knowledge**

Demonstrate some of the musical exercises that you use to practise your skills

Talk about your instrument and why you enjoy playing it (or the songs you sing and why you enjoy singing them)

Talk about several well-known pieces of music associated with your instrument or chosen songs.

☐ **Interest**

Talk about your own interests in music, including what you listen to most, and how this is similar to or different from the music you play or sing.

Musician 4

Complete ALL of the following:

☐ **Skill**

Achieve Grade Three or Four of the Associated Board of the Royal School of Music (or similar) on the instrument of your choice by singing.

☐ **Performance**

Sing or play three different types of song or tune on your chosen instrument. One should be a solo and one of the other two should accompany other musicians – you choose the music. The performance should be public, such as at a Group Show, school concert or church service.

☐ **Knowledge**

Demonstrate some of the musical exercises that you use to practise your skills.

Talk about your instrument and why you enjoy playing it (or the songs you sing and why you enjoy singing them).

Talk about some of the musicians who are associated with your instrument.

☐ **Interest**

Talk about your own interests in music, including what you listen to most, and how this is similar to or different from the music you play or sing.

Nights Away

Complete ALL of the following:

Stay away for one night, doing a Scout activity, sleeping either in tents, bivouacs, hostels, on boats or other centres.

After you've done one night away, why not work towards 5, 10, 20 or even 50!

☐ 5 Nights Away

☐ 10 Nights Away

☐ 20 Nights Away

☐ 35 Nights Away

☐ 50 Nights Away.

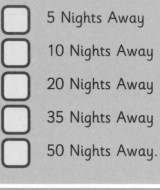

Swimmer 1

 Safety:
Know the safety rules and where it is safe to swim locally.

 Enter pool:
Without using the steps, demonstrate a controlled entry into at least 1.5 metres of water.

Short swim:
Swim 10 metres on your front.

Tread water:
Tread water for 30 seconds.

 Water skills:
Using a buoyancy aid, float still in the water for 30 seconds

Show your assessor how you can retrieve an object from chest deep water

Perform a push and glide on your front and your back.

 Distance swim:
Swim 25 metres without stopping.

 Swimming activity:
Take part in an organised swimming activity.

Swimmer 2

Complete ALL of the following:

 Safety:

Know the safety rules and where it is safe to swim locally.

☐ **Enter pool**:

Demonstrate a controlled entry or dive from the side of the pool, into at least 1.5 metres of water.

☐ **Short swim**:

Swim 10 metres on your front, 10 metres on your back, and 10 metres on your back using only your legs. Phew!

☐ **Tread water**:

Tread water for three minutes.

 Water skills:

Surface dive into at least 1.5 metres of water and touch the bottom with both hands

Mushroom float for 10 seconds

Enter the pool and push off from the side on your front and glide for five metres

From the side of the pool, push off on your back and glide for as far as possible.

☐ **Distance swim**:

Swim 100 metres without stopping.

☐ **Swimming activity**:

Take part in an organised swimming activity.

Powerpack fact

An Olympic swimming pool must be 25 metres wide, 2 metres deep and 50 metres long.

Some of the wording has been simplified. Visit www.scouts.org.uk for the original list. Speak to your Leader if there's an Activity Badge you would like to do.

Swimmer 3

Complete ALL of the following:

 Safety:

Know the safety rules and where it is safe to swim locally

Explain the rules governing swimming for Scouts.

 Enter pool:

Demonstrate a controlled entry or dive from the side of the pool into at least 1.5 metres of water.

Short swim:

Swim 50 metres in shirt and shorts.

Tread water:

Tread water for three minutes with one hand behind your back.

Water skills:

Surface dive into 1.5 metres of water and recover an object with both hands from the bottom. Return to the side of the pool holding the object in both hands.

Enter the water from the side of the pool by sliding in from a sitting position. Using any floating object for support, take up and hold the Heat Escape Lessening Posture for five minutes.

 Distance swimming:

Swim 400 metres without stopping.

 Swimming activity:

Take part in an organised swimming activity, since gaining your previous Swimming Badge.

The H.E.L.P.
-- Heat Escape Lessening Posture

This position reduces exposure of high heat loss areas of the body. Wearing a Personal Floatation Device allows you to draw your knees to your chest and your arms to your sides.

Swimmer 4

Complete ALL of the following:

☐ **Safety:**

Know the safety rules and where it is safe to swim locally

Explain the rules covering swimming for Scouts.

☐ **Enter pool:**

Demonstrate a racing dive into at least 1.5 metres of water and straddle jump into at least two metres of water.

☐ **Short swim:**

Swim 100 metres in less than four minutes.

☐ **Tread water:**

Tread water for five minutes.

☐ **Water skills:**

Surface dive into 1.5 metres of water, both head first and feet first and swim at least five metres under water on both occasions

Enter the water as for unknown depth. Swim 10 metres to a floating object and use it to take up and hold the Heat Escape Lessening Posture for five minutes.

☐ **Distance swim:**

Swim 800 metres without stopping. You should swim 400 metres on your front and 400 metres on your back.

☐ **Swimming activity:**

Take part in an organised swimming activity, since gaining your previous Swimming Badge.

Some of the wording has been simplified. Visit www.scouts.org.uk for the original list. Speak to your Leader if there's an Activity Badge you would like to do.

The Moving-On Award

About this award

You will be very busy while doing your Moving-On Award. For about four to six weeks, you will be expected to attend both Cub Scouts and Scouts. This will give you the chance to take part in meetings with the Scout Troop. This will also allow you to work towards the Scout Membership Award.

Do I have to go on my own?

It will probably be more fun if you go along to the Troop with other Cub Scouts who are also doing this badge. Your Leader will probably go with you the first time. You may see some Scouts who used to be in your Cub Scout Pack.

The Scout Leader may also come along to the Pack to meet you.

What is Scouts like?

In Scouts, just like in Cub Scouts, you will be part of a small group. This is usually called a Patrol and will often be named after a bird or animal.

The Scout Leaders or other Scouts will be able to tell you how the Scout Troop works. They may have ceremonies just like Cub Scouts. They might do some similar activities but others will be new and different.

Scouts getting ready for camp

Renewing your Promise

When you are invested as a Scout, you will renew your Promise. Your Cub Scout Leader will then be able to present you with your Moving-On Award. You can continue to wear this badge while you are in Scouts.

My Troop is called

My Troop meets at

at _____ o'clock

My Scout Leader's name is

My Scout Leader's phone number is

My Patrol is called

My Patrol Leader's name is

Finding out more about Scouts

Getting to know your Troop

→ Know and understand the Scout Promise and Law and the rules of your Troop

→ Know and understand the Scout Motto, Sign, Salute and Handshake

→ Show a general knowledge of the worldwide family of Scouting and know the meaning of the badges that you will receive

→ Know what to do at your Investiture.

Do I have to learn a new Promise and Law?

Yes. Scouts also have a Promise and Law, but the Promise is very similar to the Cub Scout Promise.

Will I have to learn another one after Scouts?

No. Everyone from Scout age in Scouting uses the Scout Promise and Law.

How can I find out more?

You can find out all you need to know, from other Scouts or your Scout Leaders.

Will I still wear a uniform?

Yes, but it will be different from your Cub Scout uniform. Instead of a dark green sweatshirt, you will wear a teal green long-sleeved shirt.

What about badges?

Scouts wear badges too. Find out what badges you will be given when you become a Scout. Ask what other badges you will be able to gain in the Scout Troop.

Getting to know your Troop

→ get to know other Members and Leaders in your Patrol and Troop

→ find out about ceremonies and traditions in your Troop

→ find out about the activities that your Patrol and Troop does.